Every Kid's Guide to
Understanding
Nightmares

Written by
JOY BERRY

CHILDRENS PRESS ®
CHICAGO

About the Author and Publisher

Joy Berry's mission in life is to help families cope with everyday problems and to help children become competent, responsible, happy individuals. To achieve her goal, she has written over two hundred self-help books for children from birth through age twelve. Her work revolutionized children's publishing by providing families with practical, how-to, living skills information that was previously unavailable in children's books.

Joy gathered a dedicated team of experts, including psychologists, educators, child developmentalists, writers, editors, designers, and artists, to form her publishing company and to help produce her work.

The company, Living Skills Press, produces thoroughly researched books and audio-visual materials that successfully combine humor and education to teach subjects ranging from how to clean a bedroom to how to resolve problems and get along with other people.

Managing Editor: Ellen Klarberg
Copy Editor: Kate Dickey
Contributing Editors: Libby Byers, Nancy Cochran, Maureen Dryden, Yona Flemming, Kathleen Mohr, Susan Motycka
Editorial Assistant: Sandy Passarino

Art Director: Laurie Westdahl
Design: Abigail Johnston, Laurie Westdahl
Production: Abigail Johnston, Caroline Rennard
Illustrations designed by: Bartholomew
Inker: Tuan Pham
Colorer: Tuan Pham
Composition: Curt Chelin

Dreams are the thoughts you have while you are sleeping. Good dreams consist of pleasant thoughts. Bad dreams consist of unpleasant thoughts.

Bad dreams are often called nightmares. They can upset you.

In **EVERY KID'S GUIDE TO HANDLING NIGHTMARES** you will learn the following:

- how nightmares affect you,
- what common nightmares are,
- how to understand nightmares, and
- how to handle nightmares.

A nightmare can make your body do strange things.
Your heart might beat faster.
You might breathe harder.

You might begin to sweat.
Your body might twitch or jerk.

A nightmare can cause you to wake up suddenly.
You might scream or call out.
You might cry.

You might forget where you are.

Nightmares can frighten you.

Nightmares can cause you to worry.

You might be embarrassed by your reactions to a nightmare.

You will feel better if you remember it is normal to
have nightmares. It is normal to react to them.
Everyone has nightmares, and everyone reacts
to them.

Other people dream many of the same nightmares you do. Here are some common nightmares:

There are many people who dream they are falling or flying.

Many people dream
- they are with other people and do not have any clothes on or
- they cannot do something they are expected to do.

There are many people who dream they are being chased by something that is going to hurt them.

Many people dream
- they cannot move or
- they are running and are not getting anywhere.

There are many people who dream
- they are threatened by a natural disaster like a tidal wave, earthquake, tornado, or flood or
- they are about to be destroyed by other disasters such as a fire, an accident, or an explosion.

Many people dream they lose something that is very important to them.

Some people dream about losing their teeth.
Some dream about losing their parents.

Sometimes you can understand your nightmares. Sometimes you cannot. This is because the things in your nightmares often stand for something else.

For example, a monster in your nightmare might mean that a person is scaring you in real life.

If something attacks you in your nightmare, it could mean that someone or something is hurting you in real life.

Your nightmares are always about you and your life.

Your nightmares are about:
- your present — something that is happening to you right now,
- your past — something that has already happened to you, and
- your future — something that is going to happen to you.

You might have a nightmare about the present. Something might happen to you while you are sleeping that will cause you to have a nightmare.

- If you are too hot, you might dream about being in a very hot place.
- If you are too cold, you might dream about doing something to get warm.

- If you are thirsty, you might dream about trying to get something to drink.
- If you have to go to the bathroom, you might dream about using the toilet. You might wet the bed.

Unusual sounds or movements that occur around you might cause you to have a nightmare.

If the wind is rattling your window, you might dream
that something is trying to get into your room
through the window.

You can prevent yourself from having nightmares about present experiences.

First, get yourself ready for bed.
- Go to the bathroom.
- Put on loose-fitting night clothes. Wear something cool if your room is hot. Wear something warm if your room is cold.

- Do not wear jewelry that can scratch or possibly choke you.
- Do not have anything in your mouth that you can swallow or choke on.
- Do not drink anything right before you go to bed or you might need to go to the bathroom in the middle of the night.

When you are ready for bed, do the following:
- Look all around your room to make sure
  it is safe.

- Turn on a small light if you feel uncomfortable in a totally dark room.
- Close your door if you want to shut out sounds that might disturb you.

- Get into bed and relax.
- Decide what you want to dream about. Choose a good dream.

You can dream only one dream at a time. If you are dreaming a good dream, you cannot dream a nightmare.

You might have a nightmare about the past. Something might not have turned out the way you wanted it to. You might still have uncomfortable feelings about it.

You might not be able to forget the experience. You might have a nightmare about it.

Here are some uncomfortable feelings that can be caused by past experiences:

Anger—feeling mad
Defeat—feeling like a loser
Disappointment—feeling let down
Embarrassment—feeling ashamed or put down
Frustration—feeling tense and discouraged

Grief—feeling sad

Guilt—feeling as if you have done something wrong

Jealousy—wishing you were like someone else

Loneliness—feeling all alone

Rejection—feeling unwanted

If these feelings are not handled in the right way, they might cause you to have nightmares.

You can prevent yourself from having nightmares about past experiences. Whenever something bad happens, try to do something about it right away.

Pay attention to your feelings and try to work them out.

If you have a hard time doing this by yourself, ask for help. Talk to someone who is old enough and wise enough to help you. Be sure it is someone you trust. Ask the person to help you solve your problems so you will not have nightmares about them.

You might have a nightmare about the future. Fear can cause nightmares about the future.

If something has hurt you, you might be afraid it will hurt you again. You might have a nightmare about it.

For example, if something painful happened when
you visited a doctor, you might be afraid about going
to the doctor again. This fear can cause a nightmare.

Worry can also cause nightmares about the future.

You might worry if you are going to do something that you do not know very much about.

If you do not know the truth about something, you might make up ideas about it. These ideas can be scary. They might cause a nightmare.

For example, if you are going to a new school that you do not know very much about, you might make up terrible thoughts about it. These thoughts can turn into nightmares.

You can prevent yourself from having nightmares about the future.

- Remember that situations change. Expect each experience to be better than the last one.
- Learn about the things that scare you. You will be less afraid of something you know about.

- Think good thoughts about your future. Try not to think terrible things are going to happen to you.
- Do not watch movies that frighten you. Do not listen to stories that scare you. They might cause you to have nightmares.

When you have a nightmare, there are several things you can do.

- Call for help, or go get help.
- Turn the light on. Look around your room to make sure that everything is OK.
- Begin thinking good thoughts.

Go back to bed when you feel better.

Try to remember what your nightmare was about.
Talk it over with someone with whom you feel
comfortable.

Be sure the person can really listen to you. The middle of the night might not be a good time to share your nightmare. The person might be too sleepy to listen.

If you pay attention to your nightmares, you will learn a lot about yourself.

If you learn to deal with your nightmares, you will make your life more pleasant.